Easy words to read
Big pig on a dig

Phil Roxbee Cox
Illustrated by Stephen Cartwright
Edited by Jenny Tyler

Language consultant:
Marlynne Grant
BSc, CertEd, MEdPsych, PhD, AFBPs, CPsychol

There is a little yellow duck to find on every page.

SCHOLASTIC INC.
New York Toronto London Auckland Sydney
Mexico City New Delhi Hong Kong

12 11 10 9 8 7 6 5 4 3   0 1 2 3 4 5/0   Printed in the U.S.A.   08   First Scholastic printing, November 2000

Big Pig gets a letter.

Look for this hat.

Big Pig

Big Pig sees the hat.

There is a map in the hat.

Big Pig runs
to Fat Cat.

4

"Fat Cat! Look at the map in this hat."

"It shows where to dig, Fat Cat."

"You dig, Big Pig. Be a pig on a dig."

7

"Let me nap

and dream of cream."

Big Pig sees three green trees.

Big Pig sees three green trees on the map.

Big Pig is happy.

He pops on a wig.

Big Pig is happy.

He hops on a twig. He can go on a dig!

"I am a happy big pig on a dig."

"I dig down

and down

and...

13

What has Big Pig found...

...down in the ground?

It's Funny Bunny.

"There's no
old gold here."

Big Pig grins. "Digging is fun too!"